IMAGES
of England

AROUND
WIRKSWORTH

Isaac Spencer, playing the euphonium at a concert in the late 1960s. He played a leading part in bringing together Brassington, Middleton and Wirksworth bands to form the BMW Band, in June 1964.

IMAGES
of England

AROUND
WIRKSWORTH

Compiled by
Denis Eardley

TEMPUS

First published 1998
Copyright © Denis Eardley, 1998

Tempus Publishing Limited
The Mill, Brimscombe Port,
Stroud, Gloucestershire, GL5 2QG

ISBN 0 7524 1192 6

Typesetting and origination by
Tempus Publishing Limited
Printed in Great Britain by
Midway Clark Printing, Wiltshire

Westbourne House, Chapel Lane, Wirksworth in the early 1900s. In 1913, it was purchased by the Marsden family, who ran the braziers and agricultural implement maker's shop in the Market Place from 1765 to 1983.

Contents

Wirksworth Market Place in the late 1930s, before the construction of Harrison Drive.

Acknowledgements

Compiling a book of this type depends very much on the generosity and interest of lots of people. The amount of help and support that I have received far exceeded my expectations, and I owe a debt of gratitude to so many people, for providing me with information, loaning photographs and other material, and spending time with me. They frequently recalled events and the names of people that had not been recorded on photographs when they were taken many years ago.

I would like to specially thank Judy Jones, not only for the photographs and material loaned, but also for the steady stream of information supplied and for her tremendous enthusiasm for the successful completion of the project.

In particular I wish to thank the following:
Kath Alesbrook, Graham Barfield, Pauline Barfield, Ellen Birch, Roy Bratby, Lynda Brewell, Joan Brown, Evie Burlinson, Chris Bush, David Bush, Steve Clamp, Judith Dean, Lance Dean, Hubert Doxey, Gillian Eardley, Bob Gerrard, Max Greatorex, Billy Gregory, Michael Handley, Joan Hatch, Daphne Heathcote, Marion Holden, Tony Holmes, Don Hughes, Chris Jones, Judy Jones, Margaret Lake, Veronica Langworthy, Keith Mellor, Roy Pearce, Cedric Pearson, Sylvia Phillips, Alan Rimmer, Ron Slack, Annie Smith, Ken Smith, Randle Tassall, Edith Taylor, Gerry Vaughan, Marion Vaughan, Mary Waterhouse, Alan Webster, Roy Webster, Doris Whitney, Alan Woolley, Bolehill W I, Community Fayre, Derby Evening Telegraph, Derbyshire Times, Wirksworth Heritage Centre, Matlock Mercury, Radio Derby.

The Heritage Centre in Wirksworth is dedicated to the collection and preservation of old photographs and memorabilia of the area and would be pleased to have the opportunity to see or hear about items that you may possess which relate to our local history. Please do what you can to help record and safeguard your heritage.

Introduction

This book provides a nostalgic look back over the last 100 years, or so, of Wirksworth and the surrounding villages. It does not attempt to tell the history of the area, but provides a wide variety of pictures, which create a vivid image of what things used to be like in times gone by. Taken together, they provide an intriguing and informative window on the social life of the area and its people, dating back to the latter part of the nineteenth century.

The pictures come from a wide variety of sources and depict the people of the area at work and leisure, from their schooldays upwards. In Wirksworth, and in many of the villages, the street scenes remain unchanged from what they were at the end of the last century. The most marked changes have been in fashion and mechanisation, both of transport and machinery. As a consequence, dramatic changes have taken place, both on the farm and in the quarry, where far fewer men are now employed.

Improvements in communications and the fact that most people now have their own motor car, or access to one, sadly have led to villages losing their shopping facilities, either in part, or altogether. Many village schools have closed, because of the declining number of children, which have made them uneconomic to sustain. All this sounds rather gloomy, but there still exists in all the villages covered by this book a strong community spirit and interest in village life with local events being well supported.

Wirksworth, standing as it does virtually at the centre of Derbyshire about two miles to the south of Peak District National Park boundary, was the centre of the English lead mining industry when it was at its height. The villages to the north and west of the town all have long histories of lead mining, while those to the south and east are predominantly farming areas. When lead mining became uneconomic, limestone quarrying took its place with all the dust, dirt, and disruption associated with it.

A road was driven through the Market Place at Wirksworth between 1938 and 1940, at the northern end to facilitate the movement of quarry traffic. The market itself was moved from its former position, close to where Harrison Drive is now situated, to the bottom of West End, following the removal of some buildings. Every Tuesday the market stalls are erected for business. Fortunately, a good number of photographs remain of the Old Market Place, which was the heart of the town, and a selection of these are reproduced in this book.

The quarrying of limestone brought with it dust, dirt, and noise on a scale never experienced before in Wirksworth. People who could afford to do so left the town; this applied to business and commerce just as much as it did to private households. Buildings became vacant and fell into disrepair. Residents began to despair of improvements ever taking place, and a once proud town began to lose confidence in the future.

In November 1978, The Wirksworth Project was launched, and there began what was a moving story of how this proud little town was restored – culminating in the award of the prestigious Europa Nostra medal in 1983, for architectural regeneration. This considerably increased the sense of pride in the town, as well as an awareness of its many attractive qualities. What was one of the finest moments in the long history of Wirksworth is recorded in this book.

On a less serious note, sport and leisure have always played an important part in the lives of the people of the Wirksworth area. Special events and trips out were eagerly awaited, and it is easy to see from the faces of those involved, on the old photographs, how much they were enjoyed. Among team sports, cricket and football were particularly popular and there was considerable local rivalry. Whether or not W.G. Grace ever played at Wirksworth Cricket Club is subject to debate, but what is certain is that the club celebrates its 150th anniversary in 1998.

I hope that this collection of pictures will bring back happy memories for many, and introduce new residents and the younger generation to an era that becomes more fascinating the more it is studied. Old photographs always produce talking points and evoke memories of people, places, and events, which, when shared, add to the enjoyment.

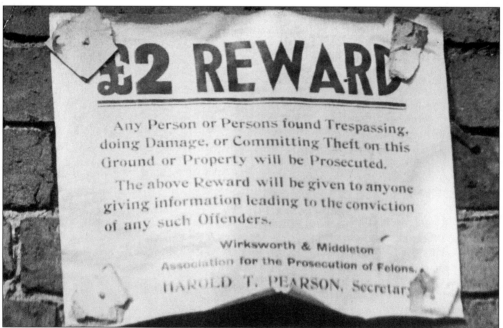

In the early 1800s, fear of Chartist unrest and the absence of any regular police force led many of the propertied and monied classes throughout the country to organise their own self-protection methods. Although the last successful prosecution was in 1935, notices were still in evidence in Wirksworth in the 1990s.

One
Wirksworth

Welcome to Wirksworth, the old lead mining capital of Derbyshire – a town that was of considerable importance, when Liverpool was a marsh, Manchester little more than a dot on the map and the great manufacturing towns of the north were in their infancy.

A market was granted by King Edward I to Thomas Earl of Lancaster, as the Lord of the Manor, in 1306, and one has been held in Wirksworth ever since. In 1938 Wirksworth saw the building of Harrison Drive, and at this time a road was built between 15 Market Place and the Red Lion Inn. Prior to this construction, the market was held in the area facing where the road now runs and is known as the Old Market Place. Next to the bank is Johnston's ironmonger's shop almost directly facing Marsdens the agricultural implement makers. The charabanc is parked in front of Watt's taxi firm and above that are Nellie Doxey's tea-rooms.

Following the construction of the new road, the market moved to the foot of West End, where it is held on Tuesday every week. It is now only a fragment of the medieval market place of old, but it still attracts plenty of interest as this late 1970s picture shows.

10

The Hope and Anchor, c. 1900. It stands on an island site within the Market Place and dates back to the seventeenth century. In the front bar is a splendid black oak fireplace overmantel with fleur-de-lys, unicorns and Tudor roses, which still remains from the original building. The shop belonging to William Wheatcroft occupied part of the building. He was a greengrocer, fishmonger and game salesman. The shop has now been integrated with the Hope and Anchor and the buildings on the right hand side at the rear were pulled down in 1938 to make way for the New Market Place.

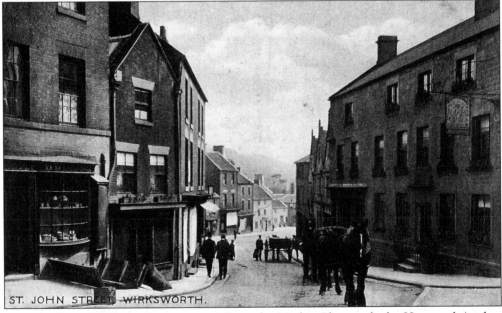

Looking down St John's Street, c. 1905, from the Market Place with the Hope and Anchor public house on the right and Hindle's chemist shop on the extreme left. Mr Wigley, a baker from Middleton, is by the cart and the two men walking down the street are Mr Middlemass, on the left, and Mr Bowmer.

Wirksworth Market Place, *c*. 1900. The celebrations taking place are reputedly for the Relief of Mafeking on the 17 May 1900.

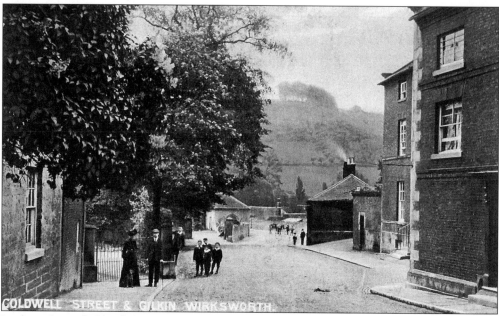

Looking down Coldwell Street towards Newbridge and the railway station, *c*. 1905. Part of the stabling block lower down the street was pulled down as a result of a road-widening scheme in the 1960s.

The Co-operative Society staff at Wirksworth celebrating their fiftieth anniversary, in front of what is now Ken's Mini Market. On the back row, from left to right: Samuel Bowyer, Alfred Bowers, -?-, Stanley Brewer, Jake Brooks, Phyllis Brocklehurst, -?-, Arthur Gratton, and Harold Spencer. On the front row: -?-, Fred Gratton, Raymond Anthony, Jack Slack, -?-, Bernard Anthony, Mr Anthony (manager), and Eddie Gell. The society premises, which began with the haberdashery section, followed round the corner into The Dale with the hardware, bread, grocery, and butcher's shop and last of all the warehouse.

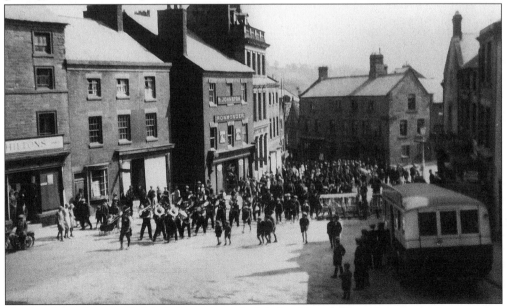

The band marching up St John's Street into the Market Place followed by a procession, on what was probably a carnival day in the 1920s.

Presentation to returning soldiers from the Boer War, which took place on Tuesday 14 October 1902. The soldiers in the front row are, from left to right: George Walton, William Goodwin, Revd Maskrey, Cob Bartlett and Mr Pearson. They were presented with cups of solid silver purchased by public subscription.

Construction work in progress on Harrison Drive, c. 1940. Although the new road improved communications, the town centre lost some of its identity as a result and became something of a wind tunnel in the winter.

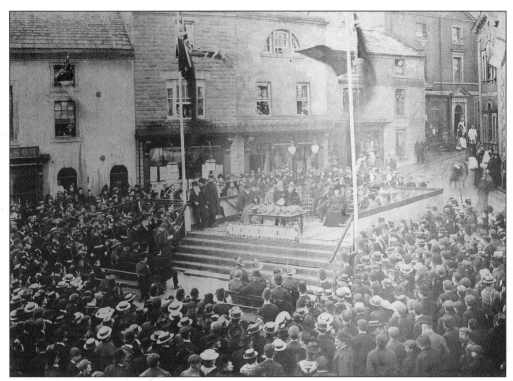

The platform erected in the Market Place for a presentation to the soldiers returning from the Boer War, in 1902. A public holiday had been declared for the occasion. The organising committee consisted of Dr A.E. Broster, Mr G. Marsden, Mr A. de Severne, as well as councillors: J. Walker JP, G.W. Walker and C. Barker, and Messrs Tait and J.K. Fritchley.

Cromford Road, before the First World War.

An early 1890s ceremony in the Market Place, probably club day.

A crowd in the Market Place, probably a 1920s carnival day. Even in those days people did not travel very far and the carnival was looked on as a very important event in the local calendar.

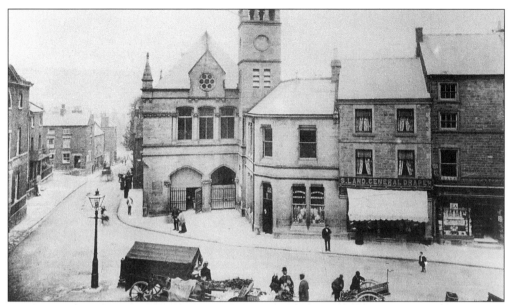

The town hall building is of Italianate design and the foundation stone was laid in 1871. It was officially opened in 1873. The area behind the arches was built as a butter market but was never used as such. The shops are, from left to right: Atkins the grocers, S. Land the draper, George Marsden the stationer, an estate agent, a publisher (postcards) and a surveyor. James Watterson's music shop juts out into the road in Coldwell Street.

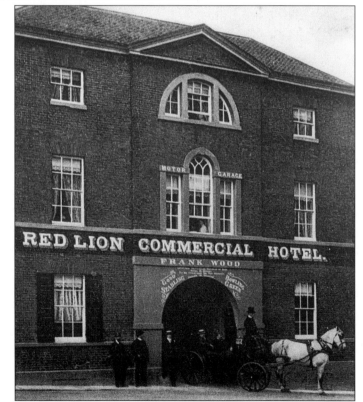

A party sitting in a carriage outside the Red Lion c. 1900. The Red Lion, is an eighteenth century coaching and posting inn, with earlier origins. The large room on the first floor with a Venetian window, over the entrance to the coach yard, was at one time used as an assembly room for important local events.

The Greatorex family shop in Coldwell Street, *c.* 1890. The shop has been in the family name since it was purchased by Benjamin Greatorex in the late 1860s at an auction sale held at the George Hotel, Wirksworth.

Waltham House, in this picture taken around 1930, was built in the early 1800s. The Wheatcroft family, who produced tape at Haarlam and Speedwell Mills, occupied it for many years. It became a cottage hospital in 1928 and is now a medical centre.

Wirksworth Hall, an eighteenth century building, was the home of Charles Hurt and his wife Susannah before eventually being sold by one of their descendants in 1858, to Nicholas Wood. Early in the 1900s, the Wood family moved to Henley Hall in Shropshire taking the wrought iron gates by Robert Bakewell with them. The house was sold around 1918 to a local person and demolished in the early 1920s due to subsidence, as the north-east corner had been built over an old mine. The lower house, now known as the Old Manse, the stables and coach house in Blind Lane are all that have survived.

The Priest's House was built around 1600. It stood at the south end of Blind Lane and was demolished in 1956. It was one of the earliest of its type in the country, but all that remains today are the stone steps that led to the first floor doorway.

Hopkinson's House, Green Hill, *c.* 1970. Before the Wirksworth Project, the house had become a ruin. The building had lost its roof in the 1950s and the walls were crumbling and the centre was filled with rubble. However, this seventeenth century, former lead merchant's house, situated only just off the Market Place was an essential part of the townscape and its restoration was vital to the successful completion of the project.

Babington House on Green Hill, *c.* 1900. It dates from about 1590. It was at one time an old workhouse, and later became a private dwelling, before eventually being converted into a cottage hospital by Miss Georgina Hurt. It is now a private residence.

One of Wirksworth's finest moments took place in June 1983, when it was presented with the prestigious Europa Nostra Award for architectural conservation. From left to right: Gordon Michell (project leader), Michael Middleton (civic trust director), and Hubert Doxey (chairman of the Wirksworth Project), receiving the award from Europa Nostra representatives. The judge presented the award, the only one to be handed to a UK project in the current series of awards. It was given for its 'exemplary regeneration of a small country town through a broad programme of self-help and innovative features'. A proud moment in the history of Wirksworth!

Looking down Green Hill in recent times with No. 13, the former home of Roy and Frances Bratby in the foreground on the left. The effect of the Wirksworth Project on Hopkinson's House at the bottom of Green Hill can clearly be seen.

Arthur Gratton, outside Sammy Buxton's house, on Green Hill around 1930. He was a baker at the Co-op bakery at the bottom of The Dale.

A gathering of post office workers and staff outside the post office, probably in the 1890s. The earliest record of the post office in Wirksworth is 1792, when Samuel Taylor held the post of receiver.

Hatfield Farm, off North End, with an ex-army vehicle in the shed, photographed around 1948. Hatfield Farm was a working farm until recent years. In 1867, it had its land severed from the house and farm buildings by the arrival of the railway.

Members of Wirksworth UDC in 1973. This photograph was taken before the re-organisation of local government in the following year, when control of most of the town's services was transferred to the newly formed West Derbyshire District Council. The councillors on the back row are, from left to right: Dennis Kneebone, Fred Spencer, Roy Barnes, Malcom Hitchcock, Mary Waterhouse, John Webster, Charles Brown JP, Joe Gould JP, and Bernard Trueman. On the front row: John Todd (public heath officer), Joe Cresswell JP (vice chairman), Hubert Doxey MBE JP (chairman), Derek Newbury (clerk to the council), and John Renshaw (treasurer).

A gathering of councillors and local people celebrating the completion of the Lady Flatts Water Scheme on 14 September 1954, which for the first time provided an adequate supply of water to Wirksworth. The water was pumped from the Blobber mine to the reservoir in Wash Green. An interesting entry in the council records for 1913 relating to the scarcity of water announced that the town crier would be sent around the town warning people against wasting water and watering gardens. On the front row, from left to right: Maurice Snow, Alderman Norman Gratton (chairman of Derbyshire County Council), Fred Slater, Mrs Gratton, Miss Harrison, Norman Harrison (chairman of Wirksworth UDC), and Jack Taylor (public heath officer).

Miss Dora Conway of Bolehill, who later moved to Cavendish Cottages on Cromford Road, Wirksworth. She started a nursing career at Derbyshire Royal Infirmary, before eventually taking up a post in Palestine. The photographer in this case was from Jaffa in Palestine and the photograph was presumably used to send home.

Adam Bede cottage, once the home of Samuel and Elizabeth Evans who were immortalised as Adam Bede and Dinah Morris in the novel, *Adam Bede*, by George Eliot. The author was the niece of Elizabeth Evans. The cottage still stands in Derby Road, but is no longer thatched.

25

Elizabeth Evans, or Dinah Morris as she is known in the novel *Adam Bede,* was for many years a local lay preacher. The memorial tablet was erected in memory of her and her husband.

Haarlem Mill, where Samuel Evans was manager in 1814. In the late eighteenth century Sir Richard Arkwright established a Cotton Mill on the site.

The parish church of St Mary the Virgin, is one of the finest parish churches in Derbyshire. The church is built in the shape of a cross and the foundations are said to date back to about 653 with much of the present structure dating from 1272. Radical restoration was undertaken between 1870 and 1874 by Sir Gilbert Scott. In the late eighteenth century the curate, the Revd Abraham Bennett, contributed considerably to the knowledge of electrical science and wrote a book entitled *New Experiments on Electricity*, which he dedicated to the Dean of Lincoln who was a trustee of the British Museum. On the Sunday following 8 September, the ancient custom of clypping is carried out, which involves the joining of hands to completely encircle the church.

The great stone slab on the north nave aisle wall of the church attracts visitors from all over the country. It is a Saxon coffin lid which was found in 1820 over a vault containing a near perfect skeleton. Intricately carved with almost forty figures from the life of Christ, its origins date back to the eighth century, or earlier.

Bertha Boam at the rear of Nether House, when she came out of service around 1928. Nether House, which was built in the late eighteenth century, was a grand three-storey town house with a severe classical frontage. For many years it belonged to the Toplis family, but it was demolished in the 1930s.

The Gilkin. Wirksworth.

The Gilkin in the early years of this century, with the brook and railway line at the rear. The three young ladies, dressed in fashionable clothes for that era, were probably taking a walk in the Hannages.

The bridge in the picture has been blown up, but in earlier days it was very important to local people living near the top of Green Hill. It enabled them to move heavy loads up to and from Rise End, which otherwise could not be taken up the road from Wirksworth. Known as the Monkey Hole, the bridge appears to have got its name following the boast of the owner of a monkey, that the animal could retrieve a coin from anywhere. A local man took up the challenge and threw the coin over the bridge for the monkey to retrieve.

Bridge connecting road over Middlepeak Quarry, Wirksworth.

The Gate House dates from before 1586. It was refronted by Philip Gell in the 1770s.

Gorsey Bank. Wirksworth.

A view of Gorsey Bank, showing Providence Mill, c. 1905. From Gorsey Bank rises one of the two sources of the River Ecclesbourne, which is a tributary of the Derwent. The other source rises just beyond Miller's Green.

Wirksworth was the old capital of the lead mining industry in Derbyshire, before 1910. Built at the head of Ecclesbourne Valley and surrounded by hills on three sides, the bulk of the town roofscape is still the same almost a century after this photograph was taken.

An early 1900s view of Yokecliffe. Most of the land from the chestnut tree to the edge of the picture has now been built on.

The lane leading to Yokecliffe Rake, c. 1923. The farm has been demolished and houses have now been built alongside the lane.

The bride in this wedding group is Hannah Botham from Gorsey Bank and the bridegroom is Tom Middleton from Bolsover. The wedding had taken place at St Mary's church, Wirksworth, on the 7 June 1911.

Henry 'Harry' Botham at Gorsey Bank where he lived. He worked at the nearby Providence Mill.

Two
Bolehill and Steeple Grange

The Railway Inn situated on the corner of Oakerhorpe Road and the B5036, *c*. 1910. It is now a farmhouse. John Howsley is in the milk float, George Robinson, the lessee of Black Rocks Quarry is on the left, and Robert Limb, his foreman, make up the picture.

Bolehill seen from the Gilkin early in the 1900s. Olive Schreiner wrote *The Story of an African Farm*, at Bolehill on one of her visits to England before the Boer War. On visiting the village she was so impressed by it, that she took lodgings and wrote her world famous book. She likened Wirksworth, lying in the hollow of the hills, to Ladysmith. It is not surprising that Bolehill was one of the first areas in this district to achieve Conservation Area status.

The 200-years-old Miners Standard is situated in what are now called the Lanes. It is the oldest of four public houses that once existed in Bolehill and was identified as such in the 1841 census. It was first listed in 1838. The Holly Bush, situated where the stables of Bolehill House are now located, was in operation in 1841, but was not shown on the census of that year. The other public houses were the New Inn, next to the Bage Mine, and the Railway Inn, on the northern edge of the village. In recent years the Miners Standard has closed, but the former proprietors still live on the premises.

Bolehill Jazz Band, *c.* 1920.

A concert party called the Happy Wanderers was formed in Bolehill in November 1960. They went around entertaining at hospitals and old peoples' homes. On the back row, from left to right: Harry Booth Jnr, Ian Harrison, Henry Booth, Brian Vallance, John Porter, and George Doxey. On the front row: Leslie Hall, Bill Prince, and Graham Millward.

Bolehill WI choir and country-dance team at a Chatsworth rally when they won the cup, 1920s. The leader is Miss C. Beresford.

Since the War Memorial was erected and dedicated in 1925, Bolehill WI has regularly cleaned it. Here we see the WI hard at work cleaning the memorial on VJ Day 1945. In the wall on the opposite side of New Road is the Greensmith Stone named after Herbert Greensmith who sold Steephill Grange, more usually known as Steeple House, to Messers Arkwright and Co. in 1771. The house was then demolished, and the stone was used to build the cotton mill at Cromford. The Greensmith Stone was found at a later date face downwards in the cellar of 24, Steeple Grange, and built into the wall where it is now sited.

The fortieth anniversary of Bolehill WI, in 1958. Admiring the cake are, from left to right: Mrs Tracey Sheldon, Mrs Mary Hodgkinson, Mrs Pem Swift, Mrs Lily Hall, Mrs Ethel Wilson, Miss Lydia Land, Mrs Land, and Miss Beth Everett.

The celebrations for Elizabeth II's coronation in 1953. The two children are: Janet Price, left, and Jennifer Embling who won first prize at the carnival. A service was held in Bolehill chapel to celebrate the coronation on 31 May 1953. Tea and a friendly get-together in the Sunday school followed this. To mark the event a competition for the best decorated house was held in Bolehill.

A landslide at the bottom of Stoney Hill, Little Bolehill with the police inspecting the slippage, together with a number of local people, in 1947. Events of this nature were not uncommon in this area. The house in the picture still remains.

The Green and Chapel Hill, Bolehill. The chapel was built in 1823; sixteen years after the Primitive Methodist chapel movement was founded. The chapel was subsequently rebuilt in 1852 to seat 150 people, at the cost of approximately £200. Pews and modern methods of heating and lighting have now replaced the old benches.

The launch of the Bolehill WI book, *Our Village Our History*, in June 1985. From left to right: Margaret Britten, Doris Whitney, Joan Gregory, and Dorothy Illingsworth. In the acknowledgements to this comprehensively detailed and highly readable book, reference is made to the chair of the history group for her 'bullying and encouragement, and for her unflagging determination that our efforts should reach fruition'. It makes one wonder, if she had anything to do with the putting up of the sign, shown above the door, to ensure deadlines were met!

Wirksworth from Bolehill. The village takes its name from the open hearths or boles where, for 400 years, lead was smelted. The smelting of lead was carried out on the tops of hills surrounding Wirksworth, where best advantage could be taken of wind force. Bolehill has developed over the years from a cluster of miners' cottages huddled around the Bage Mine. The mine recorded its highest ever yield of lead in 1844.

A view of Steeple Grange early in the twentieth century, when the usual mode of transport was horse drawn. The first telephone exchange for the Wirksworth area was operated from one of the terraced houses on the west side of Cromford Road.

Wirksworth from Steeple Grange, around 1910. Steeple Grange is a corruption of the name Steep Hill Grange. Much of the area is now taken up by an industrial estate on the north side of Wirksworth.

Three

Industry

Stone for Architectural Purposes.

KILLER BROTHERS,
— OWNERS OF —
HOPTON-WOOD STONE QUARRIES & STEAM SAW MILLS.
MIDDLETON–BY–WIRKSWORTH, DERBYSHIRE.

HOPTON-WOOD STONE.

IN BLOCK AND SAWN SLABS FOR LANDINGS, STEPS, MONUMENTS, HEADSTONES, PAVING,&
Manufacturers of Hopton-Wood Stone Chimney Pieces, Fenders, Hearth-Stones, Sills, and
Monumental Stones, &c., &c.

Setts, Kerbing, Gravel for Asphalting or Carriage Drives. Limestone for Fluxing. Road Metal, &c

This Celebrated Stone has been supplied to the following :—

New Law Courts, London.	Clayton Church, Manchester.	Ashbourn Church.
New Council Chambers, Guildhall, London.	Harris' Free Library, Preston.	St. Mary Magdalene's Church, Lincoln.
Houses of Parliament.	Rugby School.	Cloud's House, East Knoyle.
Tower of London.	L. & N. W. Railway Co.	Southwell Minster.
London and Counties Bank.	St. Michael's Church, Coventry.	Sir Henry Allsop, Alsop-en-le-Dale.
St. Augustine's Church, London.	Water Works Offices, Nottingham.	Sir Joseph Whitworth, Darley Dale.
Fine Art Institute, Derby.	Baliol College, Oxford.	Her Grace Viscountess Ossington, Cuit
Normanton Barracks, Derby.	Keble College, Oxford.	on-Trent.
Water Works Offices, Derby.	Palace Hotel, Buxton.	
Lloyd's Bank, Birmingham.	Bass & Co.'s Offices, Burton.	

And to many of the Nobility and Gentry of England. [41]

County advertisements in 1887.

Stonemasons at Middleton, c. 1930. The Hopton Wood stone used by the masons was just as hard and reliable as any top quality marble and capable of achieving a brilliant polish. It was used to enhance buildings throughout the country, some of which are detailed in the advertisement of 1887, seen on the previous page. After the First World War an order was received for thousands of headstones for graves in France and Belgium. This meant employing masons from outside the locality to assist the existing workforce. Many came from Preston, which led to a section of the sawmill being named the Preston End. The masons seen in the picture are, from left to right: Bert Petts, Fred Fearn, Joeler Spencer, Sam Jepson, So Birley, George Brace, Harry Benyon, Arthur Cordin, Jimmy Birley, Jim Spencer, Will Brace, Ike Harrison, -?-, Harold Holmes, Harold Killer, Laurie Petts, G.H. Goodall, Johnny Fox, Lol Spencer, Joe Sam Spencer.

Golconda Mine, c. 1938. From left to right: Chris Wigley, Alfie Fearn, Bill Greatorex, George Higton, Harold Dickens, Wilf Pearson, Reg Bacon, Viv Stevenson, Harry Allen, Les Milner, Jim Steeples (?).

Fred Repton and Jack Fearn prospecting near to Carsington village in the 1920s. They may have been searching for barytes or caulk, as the old miners called it, which for centuries lay unused on the waste heaps left by lead miners. Later fluorspar workings were developed using the waste that had been discarded by previous miners as worthless.

Some of the huge blocks of limestone, which were transported from Wirkworth to Port Talbot in South Wales in the 1960s, where they were used in the construction of the main breakwater for the new tidal harbour built for the British Transport Docks Board. Nearly 250,000 limestone blocks were required, and blasting techniques at the quarry had to be changed to meet the larger than normal size requirements. The blocks were then loaded onto special flat-bottomed railway wagons for transportation to South Wales

The sad sight of 3 Peak View, one of the derelict cottages on the verge of the quarry at the top of Green Hill. This is one of the examples of the devastation caused by quarrying so close to a densely populated area.

This Moot Hall was built in 1814, to replace the Moot Hall which used to stand in the Market Place. On the plain ashlar front wall are two large motifs depicting mining equipment. Inside is the miners' standard brass measuring dish for lead ore, which bears an inscription dating it to the reign of Henry VIII.

A lead mining demonstration outside Crown Yard, in 1988. The demonstration was part of the celebrations for the 700th anniversary of the time when laws of lead mining were written down and ratified at an inquisition, or Quo Warranto, granted by King Edward I and held at Ashbourne in 1288. The Barmote Court was set up to enforce the laws, and it is almost certainly the oldest industrial court in Britain, and possibly in the world; it still sits twice a year at Moot Hall.

James Else had a miraculous escape from death. The accident he was involved in was reported in the *Quarry Managers' Journal* in August 1921, as follows: 'James Else, a quarryman, was working in a limestone quarry when a charge of gelignite exploded prematurely, blowing a ramrod through his neck. Else, it appears, was pinned to the rock, but apparently the arteries were not injured. The ramrod which was of steel and was 10ft or more in length, passed halfway through Else's neck, and before he could be taken to hospital the bar had to be cut through, close to the flesh at the front and back of the neck'. Mr Else made a satisfactory recovery. The picture shows Mr J.Wardman the brother-in-law of Mr Else, who was also a quarry-man.

The quarry from the top of the Dale, in June 1968. Dust created a long-standing problem, blocking drains and making buildings dirty inside and out. Quarry lorries created noise and danger on the narrow streets, as well as spreading dirt, causing vibration damage and keeping people awake at night.

A group of workers outside the colour works in the Via Gellia. While it was common for workers in those days, without modern shower facilities, to go home covered in black or white dust, these workers went home covered in red dust from the powder they worked with.

Quarrymen at Bowne and Shaw's, Stoneycroft Quarry, in the 1920s. The railway line in the picture linked the quarry to the main line by the means of a tunnel under the town.

The quarryman's 'House Place', as it is represented at the Heritage Centre. The Heritage Centre provides a place where the history of Wirksworth's industries and people is told in a very entertaining and informative manner.

One of W.H. Phillips' lime spreading vehicles, spreading lime on farm land to improve crop growth. They travelled to many different parts of the country on contract work.

Four

Transport

The last commercial service train on the Cromford High Peak Railway, descending Hopton Incline on 21 April 1967. This was not the last train, however, and the final journeys made on the line before closure were a series of excursions, which took place north of Middleton on Sunday 30 April. They brought to an end what had been an enterprise of considerable engineering skill and ingenuity when work began in 1825. The line opened for business in 1830 and linked Cromford Wharf to Whaley Bridge, reaching a height of 1,264 feet at one point.

An ex-North London railway train 0-6-0T, LMSR 27521 lying in the road below the embankment approaching Hopton Incline, after derailment on 6 October 1937. The driver, Mr Boden, was killed in the accident.

| H 48 | WEEKDAYS | DUFFIELD AND WIRKSWORTH |

DOWN

			H	H	J			UP		J	G	J	J
			5.40 am from Chaddesden	8.20 am from Chaddesden						To Chaddesden	EBV	To Chaddesden	To Chaddesden
			52	39	39					52	39	39	39
Mileage					SX Q PM		Mileage				SX Q PM	SO PM	SX PM
M	C		am	am			M	C		am			
0	0	DUFFIELD .. .. arr	..	9 10	..	..	0	0	WIRKSWORTH .. dep	10 40	12 30	5 5	7 40
		.... dep	6 18	9 14	1 40	....	3	32	Idridgehay	10 52	12 40	5 18	7 58
3	35	Shottle .. .. arr	..	9 26	..	....	4	74	Shottle .. .. arr	10 58	..	..	..
		.... dep	..	9 42	....	....			.... dep	11 0	..	..	..
4	77	Idridgehay	6 36	..	..	....	8	29	DUFFIELD .. .. arr	11 18	12 58	..	8a20
8	29	WIRKSWORTH.... arr	6 53	10 10	2 20	....			.... dep	11X23	..	5X35	8a40
										GL		GL	

Timetable for the Duffield and Wirksworth train services for the period from September 1956 to June 1957.

Engine number 26428, standing at Black Rocks sidings in Spring 1948. On the footplate from left to right: fireman Bill Lowe, and driver Jack Harrison. On the step: Dennis Vallance. On the ground: -?-, Lionel Brookes, Sam Hall and Herbert Hallows.

Cromford High Peak Railway staff, all ready to go for the last day of commercial service on the line in 1967. From left to right: guard Arthur Millward, driver Sam Buckley and fireman Dennis Vallance at Middleton Top. These three men were affectionately known locally as the Three Musketeers.

Wirksworth Railway Station, with Samuel Hodgkinson, the station-master on the footplate, in 1874. The station was opened in 1867, when the railway came to town linking Wirksworth with Derby and markets far beyond that, through the rapidly expanding national rail network. It opened up tremendous opportunities to improve the sales and distribution of limestone. In 1879 a tunnel was constructed under the town, linking the station with Dale Quarry to streamline still further the movement of limestone.

An Austin taxi run by Edwin Webster and Sons of Hognaston, *c.* 1928. In emergencies the taxi was used at any time of day or night, both to take people to hospital and to transport doctors to patients.

E. Webster and Sons, Garner R 7923 bus, in St John's Street, Wirksworth in the early 1920s. Edwin Webster Jnr stands at the front. The firm's first merchandised vehicle to take the road shortly after the First World War was a Ford Model T convertible lorry/bus, but late in 1921 came the real changeover to motor vehicles when a Garner 15 bus/van R7923 was purchased. It was able to carry 21 passengers or 30 cwt of goods, and cost £855, complete.

Bedford OB model, the workhorse of the Webster Fleet, outside the vehicle repair depot in Hognaston, c. 1946. The depot also sold petrol and owned the only pump in the village.

Webster's garage, which was used for their buses in the main street, Hognaston in the early 1950s. The garage was demolished in the 1990s after the sale of the business. Records show that the Webster family was involved in transport as far back as 1666, when trains of packhorses were used. At the beginning of the century Edwin Webster was in business as a carrier using a horse drawn van to carry passengers and different kinds of goods.

Roy Bratby of Wirksworth, at army camp, riding on a BSA Blue Star motor bike in 1940. Note the mask on the lamp, which was used during wartime to conform to lighting regulations.

Miss Prince from The Study, Bonsall, out for a ride with her dogs, early in the 1900s. At a later date she acquired a Rolls Royce, and when the children in the village saw her coming down the drive they would rush to open the gate and get a penny or two reward for their efforts.

Pictures are not always what they seem! This is not, as it appears to be, a picture of three ladies out for a spin in the Peak District, but a photograph taken in a photographer's studio on a visit to Blackpool in 1942. The 'travellers' are, from left to right: Ethel Webster, Annie Webster, her mother, and Mabel Webster (no relation) all from Wirksworth.

The annual Christmas dinner dance of W.H. Phillips Limited, haulage contractors at the Town Hall, Wirksworth, in the early 1960s. In the foreground are Mr and Mrs Cliff Brookes, Mr and Mrs Raymond Mellor, Mr and Mrs Stuart Bramwell, Mr and Mrs John Jones, and Mr and Mrs Weiton. One mine company had a fleet of around 200 vehicles and always gave strong support to Wirksworth Carnival by providing transport for the floats.

These motorbike riders in Hillside Lane, Brassington, are Jack Spencer, on the left, and John Handley, *c.* 1932. Jack Spencer's father was a butcher in Brassington and John Handley's father was coal merchant.

Five

School and
Teenage Days

Anthony Gell school on the day of the charity walk to Duffield and back, in September 1966.
This was the start of the second year under the Comprehensive Education system and the first
year that the whole school joined together on one site.

Newbridge secondary modern school, High Peak sports team when Mr J. Cresswell was headmaster, in 1959. On the front row, from left to right: Sylvia Bateman, Kay Williams, Margaret Hunt, Ann Brewell, Margaret Hallows, Barbara Jones, Kay Thompson, Shirley Morris, Joan Slack, Joan Marchington.

Wirksworth Junior school, c. 1954. On the back row, from left to right: Roger Southam, Michael Webster, Pamela Boden, Carol Fletcher, Ken Oxspring, Ann Batterley, Rodney Spencer, Lynn Clacher, Rodney Henshall, Jean Houghton, Margaret Cowlishaw, Nigel Williams, and David Burton. On the middle row: Joe Bradley, Paul Ogden, Kathleen Batterley, Linda Gratton, Pat Wain, Neville Taylor, Gerald Booth, Lynda Allsop, Martin Mitchell, and John Noble. On the front row: David Harbison, Laurence Redfern, Peter Hall, Tom Smith, Arthur Hitchcock, Carl Taylor, Raymond Ranger, David Higton, Jim Gallimore, and Chris Mordey. The teacher is Ivan Baldwin.

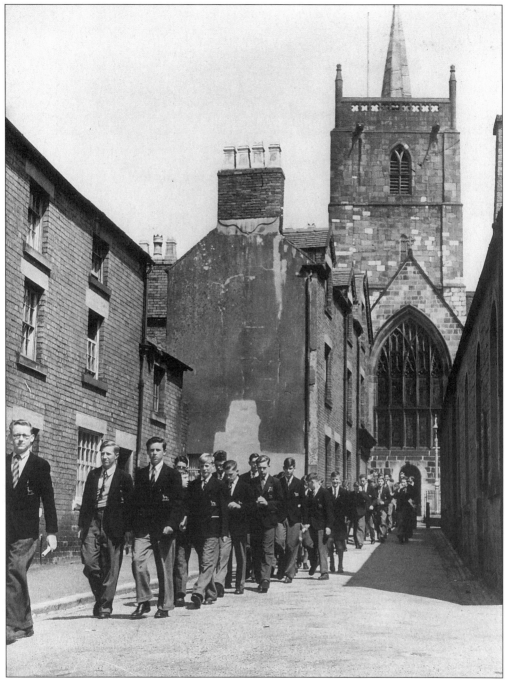

Third year pupils from Anthony Gell school, leading the way down St Mary's gate from the church on Founder's Day 10 July 1952. The school was founded in 1576.

A group of girls from Anthony Gell school, *c.* 1934. On the back row, from left to right: Joan Stevenson, Joan Parker, Monica Hargreaves, Mary Slater, Eileen Britland, Mary Doxey, Margery Rains, and Hilda Petts. On the third row: Muriel Best, Jeanne Woodward, Gwen Merrill, Dorothy Cappendell, Gwen Moore, Edith Stanley, and Joan Bingley. On the second row: May Slater (only part) Andrea Howe, Mary Oldfield, Kathleen Read, Ruth Buckland, Beth Bowmer, and Rene Dyer. On the front row: Ethel Hawley, -?-, Kathleen Harrison, Kathleen Crofts, Evelyn Stamp, Peggy Rush, and Joyce Seeds.

The senior girls hockey team, Anthony Gell School, in 1954. On the back row, left to right: Linda Wright, Ann Croft, Doreen Measham, Miss Wildgoose (PE teacher), Janet Robinson, Tessa Spencer, Noreen Cave. On the front row: Betty Bembridge, Margaret Spencer, Joyce Mee, Valerie Hallows, Ann Cole, and Norma Spencer. They were photographed in the school quadrangle.

A group of boys and teachers from Anthony Gell school, in 1934. On the back row, from left to right: Charlie Marsden, Dennis Rains, John Bowmer, Roy Bratby, Fred Richardson, Trevor Petitt, and Ernest Price. On the third row: Dick Smith, ? Read, Jesse Cordin, Norman Webster, Ivor Hibbert, Harold Farnsworth, and Denzil Hazard. On the second row: Miss Janus, Mr Holroyd, Bill Walker, George Evans, Don Dakin, and Leslie Houghton. On the front row: Tom Smedley, Edward Howard, Norman Ferguson, Michael Bowmer, and John Payne.

The Hannages, *c.* 1961. This picture was taken before the land was acquired for playing fields, for the Anthony Gell school. From left to right: Alan Woolley, John Seeds, Ian Chalmers, Jed Bunting, Bill Mather, and Ken Slack.

This is not the new school uniform, but Wirksworth junior school children preparing for a concert in 1947. On the back row, from left to right: teacher (name not known), Marlene Talbot, Marilyn Cresswell, Judith Hitchcock, -?-, Linda Hodgkinson, Keith Mather, Pete Haworth, Dan Doxey, Stuart Sims, Clayton Slack, and -?-. On the front row, Madge Oliver, Ivan Fearn, Geoff Buckley, Alan Woolley, Ann Wilson, Nancy Wood, Joy Fearn, Alice King, -?-, and Pat Colebourne. At the front is John Chadwick.

Members of Wirksworth youth club in the mid 1950s. They are seen at the memorial Hall with the leader Des Marsden seated at the table.

Six

Sport and Leisure

Wirksworth St Mary's football team in the 1901/2 season. On the back row, from left to right: J. Porter, J. Brough, C.W. Taylor, W. Wain, and L. Hanson. On the middle row: R. Limb, W.A. Bowmer, R. Wall, A. Wardman, W.T. Taylor, and B. Hilditch. On the front row: A. Hatfield, and W. Woodhouse.

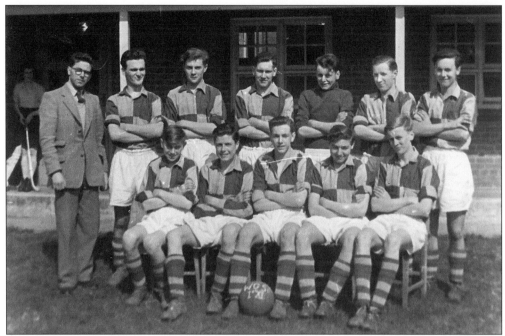

The senior boys football team, from the Anthony Gell school, in 1954. On the back row, from left to right: Jack Rodgers, Mick Rowbotham, Mick Hall, Barry Doxey, Mick Holt, Geoff Buckley, and Lance Dean. On the front row: Peter Bates, Norman Simpson, Ian Buxton (captain), Ray Taylor, and Peter Haworth. Ian Buxton later played both for Derby County and Derbyshire County Cricket Club.

Wirksworth Ivanhoe football team, pictured at their Recreation Road ground in the early 1960s. On the back row, from left to right: Lance Dean, Charlie Hallows, Peter Brewell, Marcus Hallows, Richard Needham, and Gorden Slack. On the front row: John Linthwaite, Keith Gell, Brian Wanford, Bill Mather, and Gerald Bunting. In the 1961/62 season Wirksworth Ivanhoe won the Matlock and District League Cavendish Cup.

Wheatsheaf public house football team, pictured on the Hannages, c. 1950. On the back row, from left to right: Dennis Osbourne, John King, George Taylor (publican), Bill Lobby, Derek Moxon, and Tom Matkin. On the front row: Mac Wilkinson, Frank Doxey, -?-, Reg Knighton, and Bernard Waterhouse.

Wirksworth Cricket Club team in the 1911 season. The distinction of playing the first recorded match in Derbyshire belongs to 'eleven young men from Wirksworth against eleven from Sheffield for £50 aside'. The result was disputed, but the money was awarded to the Wirksworth team. Wirksworth Cricket Club was established in 1849, and home matches have been played from that date onwards, on its ancient Recreation Road ground.

Wirksworth Cricket Club, in the 1930s. On the back row, from left to right: Alec Slater, Ron Farrell, (who ran a popular dance band in Wirksworth), Ken Jones (umpire), Jack Williams, Les Walker, and Bill Webster. On the middle row: Bill Thompson, Noel Radford, and Claude Brooks. On the front row: Philip Ogden, Jack Marsden (an ironmonger in the Market Place), Frank Clay, and Fred Read (who ran a general store at the top of St John Street).

The Wirksworth Girl Guides in 1956. They are, back row, left to right: M. Yeomans, M. Wilson, J. Andrews, K. Robinson, M. Hartle, J. Wright, E. Hopkins, J. Brooks, V. McLean, J. Biddle, A. Simmons, R. Stafford. Middle row: J. Holmes, S. Slack, C. Ormond, P. Draycott, J. Eyre (Company Leader), Miss Northrop, J. Palin, P. Hawkins, J. Harrison, J. Coley, A. Cowley. Front row: P. Wain, M. Empringham, L. Gratton, C. Freeman, L. Allsop, B. Longbottom, M. Rowbottom, R. Grassby, J. Vallance, G. Hickton, K. Kirk.

The Old Wirksworthians ladies hockey team, who played their home matches on the Anthony Gell school field, c. 1960. The team was much respected by local rivals and usually won most of their matches by a clear margin. On the back row, from left to right: Valerie Hallows, Dorothy Brewell, Agnes Fidler, Nora Wibberley, Ann Cowley, and Annie Webster. On the front row: Mary Buxton, Eileen Brewell, -?-, Norma Spencer, and Gillian Brace.

Tennis at the Malt Shovel, in the 1900s. It would appear that a mixed doubles game is about to start for the attentive spectators in the background. The tennis court is now a car park. Around 1918 the Malt Shovel gained an increase in customers following the closure of the nearby Noah's Ark Inn.

Bathing in a quarry, near Harborough Rocks, known locally as the Bees' Nest. Apparently some of the young men in the picture could not swim. They are, from left to right: Jim Ferris, Jack Spencer, and Reg Dakin, with Cyril Brindley in front.

Members of the cast of *Emma* by Jane Austen, which was performed at Anthony Gell school during the 1956/57 school year. On the back row, from left to right: Allan Clark, David Shaw, Marion Davis, Michael Gill, L. Jordan, Diana Dunn, Patricia Humphries, Annette Hudson, and Tom Larimore. On the front row: John Grundy, Patricia Hawkins, Elizabeth Bembridge, Stephen Wright, Monica Webster, John Talbot, and Margaret Richards.

Constance Bratby, who the took part of the native girl, in the *Desert Song* at Matlock Cinema, in the 1930s.

Farmers from Wirksworth and District, visiting Lever Brothers Ltd corn and fertiliser factory, at Port Sunlight in 1937. For many of them who did not normally travel far from Wirksworth, this was the highlight of the year.

Wirksworth ladies enjoying the bracing sea air at Skegness, in 1952. The day trip had been organised by the George Hotel for 'ladies only'. All the ladies took some type of musical instrument with them and paraded on the promenade to entertain holidaymakers. They were, from left to right: Gladys Thompson, Violet Hodgkinson, Mary Waterhouse, Eva Walker, Violet Carter, Lillian Else, Mary Armitt, and Florence Dean.

An attentive audience at Wirksworth Town Hall cinema when a number of people had to stand at the rear, in 1947. The cinema was run by J. 'Freddie' Slater and was obviously a very popular form of entertainment.

Coronation celebrations at Gorsey Bank, in 1953. The group of happy partygoers paraded behind a band travelling around Wirksworth. They later took part in a comic football match. On the front row, from left to right: J. Goodhead, D. Petts, E. Wilde, G. Gration, L. Taylor, L. Else, and M. Waterhouse. On the back row: G. Thompson, F. Barlow, N. Gration, I. Fearn, I. Brace, M. Armitt, E Armitt, W. Thompson, D. Marsh, B. Waterhouse, A. Bunting, and R. Thompson.

Crowning the carnival queen, *c.* 1938. This event took place at Wirksworth Hospital Carnival on the recreation ground. Before the National Heath Service came into existence, local people raised substantial sums of money for their hospitals at carnivals.

The first pageant to be held in Wirksworth, when Dr Broster of Coldwell Street undertook the organisation and the writing of the script, *c.* 1947. A great deal of time and care was taken in making the fairies' outfits and for the residence at the rear, with its thatched roof and paper flowers adorning the walls.

Mr L. Hanson and his wife at the centre of a merry costumed group, celebrating at Wirksworth Hospital Carnival, *c.* 1938.

The Carnival Queen, Rebecca Thorpe, and her retinue awaiting the arrival of HM Queen Elizabeth II on her visit to Wirksworth in 1992. They were, from left to right: Amy Wardman, Louise Spencer, Stephanie Andrews, Debbie Spencer, Rebecca Thorpe, Danielle Guise, Richard Maskery, Joanna Ward, Paul Wilkinson, and Joanna Baker. Of these ladies in waiting, Joanna Baker later became Queen of Derbyshire and Danielle Guise became Junior Queen of Derbyshire.

The town crier, Walter Green, who was the landlord at the Hope and Anchor, leading the band up St John Street, *c.* 1985. The town crier's role is now only a ceremonial one, but in the past, the council used to send him around the town to announce important news and to give warnings. Older inhabitants can remember when the town crier, Luther Gould, went around warning that the water was going to be cut off, which used to be a fairly regular occurrence, even in summers that were not excessively dry.

The W.H. Phillips carnival float won first prize in 1970. Derby County, or the 'Rams' as they are frequently called, had just won promotion to the old First Division of the Football League and the float celebrated their success. They even went to the extent of having a live ram on board. On the float are, from left to right: Dennis Phillips, Chris Phillips, Stephen Phillips, David Greenhough, Graham Clay, Roy Phillips, Geoff Phillips, and Chris Pugh.

Cyclists testing their speed and strength in the climb up West End, as part of the Milk Race Tour of Britain. Wirksworth has always been a popular place for testing body and machine. It was in 1912 that Rolls Royce tested cars on Green Hill, prior to entry into the Austrian alpine trials. The trials were a great success for Rolls Royce and they came back from Austria with the prestige of the company considerably enhanced.

The Well that won first prize, in 1914. Wirksworth well dressing in its present form began as a dressing of public taps in 1827, as a thanksgiving for piped water.

An outing to Blackpool in the late 1930s to celebrate the marriage of Malcom Wheatcroft. He was the son of the owner of Haarlam Mill, and married Peggy Allsopp of Slayley Hall, Slayley, Bonsall.

'Fight the good fight', one of Wirksworth's best remembered well dressings, for the magnificence of its design.

Seven
Amber Valley Villages

Alderwasley Hall, built in the late eighteenth century with nineteenth century additions, was the home of the Hurt Family until it was sold in 1930. Since then it has been put to various educational uses. The Hurts came to the village in 1670 following the marriage of Nicholas Hurt to the sister and heiress of John Lowe, whose ancestors had been lords of Alderwasley since 1471. Apart from being substantial landowners, the Hurts were involved in lead smelting at one time. Timber also produced a lucrative income for the family, particularly in the eighteenth century. Alderwasley was the most profusely wooded of all the Derbyshire parishes, as it had once formed part of the Duffield Frith, which was one of the county's two royal forests.

Alderwasley post office *c*. 1968. It operated from Pendleton Cottage Farm from 1965 until closure in 1987. It is now a private house and there is no longer a post office in the village.

In the turnip fields at Broadgates Farm, Ashleyhay, in the 1950s. From left to right: Oswald Slack, Reg Rumbelow (who was from Cardiff and was helping out on the farm during his holidays), Dorothy Slack, Joan Slack and a horse named Jim. Ashleyhay is a scattered farming village, with a population of 110, as recorded in the 1991 census.

Packhorse Farm, Alderwasley on the corner of Jackass Lane and Wirksworth Road, in the early 1900s. This was once the main packhorse route between Wirksworth and Nottingham. Lead was carried to Nottingham, and frequently bones were brought back for crushing at the mill at Wiggonlea Farm to be used as fertiliser on the land.

Haymaking at Broadgates Farm, Ashleyhay, in 1954. Oswald Slack is on the cart, with farm-hands Joe and Harry Oakes, who both came from a local farming family. Nowadays, haymaking is more mechanised and many farmers have turned to the silo, which avoids the necessity of having to rely on fine weather to gather the crops.

The Alderwasley Agricultural and Horticultural Show presentation ceremony, in the 1950s. The cup that has been awarded to Mr Slack was probably for the prize potatoes which he grew on his farm. The lady on the right has been awarded the cup in the housewives' section of the show. Also in the picture are Mr Chadfield (chairman of the Parish Council), and his wife, Joan Gregory who ran the WI, Ted Bunting (blacksmith), Frank Cooper (farmer), Mr and Mrs Pickering with their daughter, Mrs Crookes and her daughter.

Alderwasley church, c. 1908. The church was built by F.E. Hurt at a cost of £2,300 and was opened in 1850. Few churches in England can be in such a delightful setting, just within the gates of the beautiful park belonging to Alderwasley Hall. A cedar tree stands guard, while just below, a sparkling stream runs with little waterfalls and ornamental lakes.

St Margaret's village hall, Alderwasley, viewed from the north west. It was originally a chapel and was converted to its present use in about 1982. A chapel existed on this site at least as far back as 1531.

Alderwasley school before the First World War. It is now a private house.

Pupils at Alderwasley school, in about 1916. Miss Bunting was the headteacher at the time, but is not shown in the photograph. The school was erected in 1841 for sixty children and formally opened in 1843. It was enlarged to accommodate one hundred children in 1897, but it closed its doors in 1970.

Alport Stone, c. 1952. This massive gritstone monolith stands on Alport Heights which rise to 1,032ft above sea level. This hilltop, covering nine acres of land, was given to the National Trust in 1930 and represents the first acquisition by the Trust of a scenic nature in Derbyshire.

A sign advertising Ye Olde Bear Inn, a mid eighteenth-century public house at Alderwasley. An unusual feature, in the present day, is the existence of a helicopter pad at The Bear, as it is now commonly known in the area.

An early 1900s view of Station Lane, Idridgehay, which was once a regular meeting point for farmers who brought their milk to the station for transportation to London and Sheffield. The line opened in 1867, but closed for passenger service in 1948, although it was still used occasionally for mineral trains and excursions. The stationmaster's house, built in 1867, still remains, but has now been converted into a private house.

Alton Manor Festival, where every year the Normandy Veterans Association meet to plant an oak tree as a memorial to lost colleagues. The manor is situated one mile north of Idridgehay and was built in 1846 by Sir Gilbert Scott with stone quarried in the grounds.

Looking across the lake to Alton Manor, in the early 1900s. Three people are enjoying a boating trip on the lake, while another looks on.

A view of St James church, Idridgehay, from the main Derby to Wirksworth Road, before the Second World War. The church, which occupies a prominent main road site, was built by Henry Isaac Stevens of Derby in 1885–6.

The vicarage at Idridgehay, *c.* 1916. It was demolished after being damaged by a mine dropped from a German bomber plane in the Second World War.

Derby Road, Idridgehay, *c.* 1910.

Eight
Bonsall, Via Gellia and Ible

People admire the well dressing at the bottom of Church Street, Bonsall, in 1961. The dressing of wells, which began in the village along with the carnival in 1927, usually takes place on the last Saturday in July. The shaft of the Market Cross dates back to the fourteenth or fifteenth century but the ball head was added in 1671. Miss Prince of The Study paid for the shaft to be restored in 1871.

St James church choir, Bonsall around 1936. On the back row, from left to right: Winnie Swift, Mary Young, Mary Westerman and Edith Prince. In the middle row: Majorie Potter, Alan Smith, Herbert Poundall, James Shackley, William Gregory, William Poundall, Arthur Potter, Hilda Prince, Sam Davis, and Majorie Harrison. In the front row: Doris Marshall, Elsie Alsebrook, Edith Taylor, Lucy Sheldon, Revd J.B. Bunting, Anne Redfern, Margaret Knowles, Lucy Plant, and Nellie Plant.

The Pig of Lead Inn, with the crushing plant and quarry behind. They were linked by a light railway line in the early 1920s. The house at the rear belonged to the Axe family, who owned the quarry. Although the claim may be disputed, *The Daily Mail* once called Bonsall 'the healthiest village in England', because of the long life spans of its inhabitants, who were kept fit by climbing its long steep streets. From The Pig of Lead to the upper end of the village it is a climb of 450 feet. The Pig of Lead closed a few years ago and is now a private house.

George Axe and his sister, Judith, in Ember Lane, Bonsall, in 1955. The parish church of St James, in the background, is over 700 years old and it is quite probable that a wooden church existed before the stone one. An unusual feature in the church is the presence of a bullring, which was referred to in the following story from the *Derbyshire Courier* of 2 August 1834. In an article about bull baiting, it said, 'At the Bonsall Wakes on Monday last, thirty to forty men had gathered with dogs, and clubs ... the worthy clergyman remonstrated with the men in vain ... he purchased the release of the animal for one guinea'. Apart from saving the bull, presumably the vicar's purchase included the bullring itself, which if this story is correct accounts for its presence in the church.

A gathering of Bonsall folk watching the banner being held aloft in a celebration, in the early 1900s. The Queen's Head Inn is behind the cross, which was once the centre of a thriving market place.

Broth eating on Wakes Thursday, on the steps of the cross. Little appears to be remembered now of the origin of what was a popular annual custom up to the early 1900s.

Costumed revellers celebrating the 300th anniversary of the Kings Head in 1977. The inn's first landlord was Anthony Abell and the same family ran it until the 1890s.

Bonsall Church of England school, *c.* 1928. In the back row, from left to right: D. Alesbrook, D. Prince, L. Oliver, B. Bunting, A. Smedley, W. Swift, R. Bunting, C. Alesbrook, and Revd J.C.T. Taggart. In the middle row: I. Banks, E. Sheldon, M. Young, A. Sheldon, M. Fern, N. Spencer, I. Fern, M. Shackley, and E. Gratton. In the front row: M. Knowles, E. Gratton, D. Bunting, I. Massey, J. Brown, C. Doxey, H. Poundall, and A. Spencer. Seated: R. Stone, A. Bunting, and E. Webster.

The ladies cricket team outside the Fountain Inn, Bonsall, perhaps the forerunners to the successful English ladies cricket team that won the World Cup in 1993! The Fountain, which closed in the 1980s, was previously known as the New Inn.

The Study was the former home of the Prince family. Miss Prince died in 1927 and the house was demolished between the wars and its stone re-used elsewhere. It had attractive lawns, trees and fishponds and grapes grew in the greenhouses. Flats have now been built on this site.

Bonsall Amateurs in the 1904/5 season. Football was popular in Bonsall and at one time there were four teams that played regularly. These were: Bonsall St James, Bonsall Firsts and Bonsall Juniors. Slayley Amateurs also had a team in the early 1900s.

The Barley Mow, with the landlord John Slack outside. He ran a farm from the premises as well as a public house. In recent times the Barley Mow has been the starting place for walks around the area, led by the landlord. It has also been the venue for the World Championships for hen racing over the last few years!

Five views of the Via Gellia, *c.* 1918. The Tufa cottage is most unusual, being constructed of tufa rock formed from dissolved limestone which has been redeposited in water.

Haymaking at Slinterfields, *c.* 1912. The horses in the picture pulled the coal barges at Cromford Wharf and the men were employed by G.H. Wheatcroft.

Freda Boden on her boyfriend's motor bike in the Via Gellia, in 1926. The road was named after Philip Gell of Hopton Hall who paid to have it constructed through the valley in 1791–2, improving access between his lead mines and the lead smelter at Cromford. The trade name Viyella originates from the fabric that was once produced at the textile mill in the Via Gellia.

95

Rider Point, *c.* 1909. The long one-storey building on the left once provided refreshments for walkers and cyclists. Ham and egg breakfasts were a speciality. The Tollhouse is on the right.

The lane through Ible, in the 1960s. Often referred to as one of the last medieval hamlets in Derbyshire, this small farming community recorded a population of only thirty-nine in the last census in 1991. D.H. Lawrence wrote a short story about the village entitled *The Wintry Peacock*.

Nine
Brassington

A picture of Tudor House, taken before 1964, when the right hand side of the house was renovated. It was built in 1615, by Thomas Westerne and was called the New Hall and the date stone at the front of the house shows his and his wife's initials. Later it became the Red Lion public house and remained as such for over 150 years. It was well sited, being situated on what was at one time the main London to Manchester turnpike road. From 1820 to 1848, the building fulfilled the role of housing paupers for the Ashbourne Poor Law Union; seventy-seven names were recorded at one stage. The men were provided with work, namely breaking stone into specific sizes at the rear of the house. It only became known as the Tudor House in about 1900 and is now divided into two private houses.

Dick and Jos Taylor at the smithy in Dale End, *c.* 1900. The smithy was very much a social meeting place for local people who would swap tales, watch the horses being shod and keep warm by the fire, all at the same time.

The George and Dragon public house, *c.* 1910. Since its closure it has been converted into two dwellings, which are aptly known as Dragon House, on the left and Dragon Cottage, on the right. For a period, from 1845 to 1848, the building was used as an annexe to Tudor House to house paupers for Ashbourne Poor Law Union. This continued until, what is now, St Oswald's hospital at Ashbourne was built.

St James's church, before restoration, in 1879. The need for urgent repairs is clearly indicated by the massive crack in the front wall. The church dates back to the late twelfth century, and is Norman in origin. A carved figure on a stone inside the clock chamber indicates that worship may have been carried out here in Saxon times, or even earlier.

Maddock Lake, c. 1900. Maddock Lake formed part of the original settlement known as Maggot Lake, in the seventeenth century. The name probably came from a spring of water, which provided the permanent water supply.

Brassington Wakes Carnival in around 1935. It starts on the last Sunday in July and is followed by events throughout the week. Dressing up in fancy dress is an important part of the carnival and there are prizes for various classification winners. On the front row, from left to right: Mary Whittaker, Patricia Cooper, Margaret Tomkinson, and Pam Gould. Also included in the picture are : Mary Gerrard, Pascoe Gerrard, Vera Whittaker (LSD), Dorothy Gleeson (with a stick), Beryl Tomkinson, Freda Buckley and Mary Seals (in a white hat). The two men are probably Mr Watson and Mr Hopkins.

Brassington Band, in the 1930s. There has been a band in existence here since at least 1761, but in 1964 it amalgamated with Wirksworth and Middleton bands to form the BMW Band. The band members are, from left to right: C. Whittaker, R. Holdsworth, B. Taylor, C. Gould, -?-, -?-, F. Radford, T. Gregory, J. Warner, B. Handley, -?-, A. Highton, -?-, Mr Moss and E. Askey.

The Gate Inn was built in 1616 and substantially altered in 1874. It was the place where coachmen used to stop to quench their thirsts, and be served through a specially designed window before going on their way. On the opposite side of the road, where the post office is now, was believed to be the Tollhouse. The gate across the road probably gave its name to the public house.

Well Street, c. 1900. The butcher's shop in the centre of the picture has since been demolished, and the former thatched cottages have had an extra floor added. The Co-operative shop on the left is now the post office.

The carrier's cart viewed from the vicarage, c. 1900. The big tree is situated in the area used for many years by Brassington football club. The barn has now been converted into houses but behind it still stands the pump where animals were watered.

The Miners Arms football team between 1900 and 1910. The Miners Arms was built in 1734, and is one of the two remaining public houses in the village. The landlord from 1804 to 1860 was Thomas Slack. He was also the local Barmaster until 1839 and presided over Brassington Liberty, where lead-mining disputes were settled.

Brassington cricket team in the 1920s. On the back row, from left to right: Mr Mellor, -?-, J. Spencer Jnr, -?-, Mr Warner, and J. Spencer Snr. On the front row: A. Gould, G. Brindley, Mr Dent, B. Brindley, -?-. On ground: T. Brittain, and J. Ferris.

Brassington football team of 1928/29. On the back row, from left to right: H. Buckley (trainer), Alec Gould, Bill Brindley, Henry Woodhouse, George Brindley, George Wigley, and Ted Brittain. On the front row: Vernon Gould, Jack Brindley, J. Spooner, R. Gillot, R. Warner.

Harborough Rocks, near Brassington, *c.* 1900. Mr Gregory is standing outside the farm buildings. The High Peak Trail now runs just below the buildings pictured.

Brassington school, February 1927. The headmaster was Mr Dent.

Ten
South
Western Villages

Thornhill House, in the foreground, was built around 1880 and was the building from which Mrs Annie Stevenson conducted a catering business from 1933–87. The rectory at the rear was built in 1859, for Revd Francis Brett who was curate and then rector over a period of fifty years – a memorial tablet can be found on the south wall of the church.

A picture of Carsington taken before 1906, when Doglow Wood was planted along the line of trees seen here, on the sky-line. This tree line marks the boundary of Carsington and Hopton. To the north-west rises Carsington Pasture, which is riddled with disused lead mines. A well-known landmark to the north is the King's Chair, a limestone crag hollowed out in the shape of a throne. It was originally known as Lady Chair but was probably re-named at the time of the Reformation.

St Margaret's church, Carsington, before 1910. In 1910, stained glass windows were installed in memory of Henry and Theresa Gell. The church itself probably dates from the first half of the fourteenth century, although there is evidence that a church existed as far back as the twelfth century. It is interesting to note that in 1971, a gravedigger dug up the skeletons of a man, woman and child probably of Anglo-Saxon origin. They were sitting bolt upright with their legs outstretched. Radical alterations were carried out to the church in 1648, when the battlements were also added.

Looking across the fields from
Hopton to Callow with Hall
Woods in the background.

The Glebe House was built as a
rectory, in 1637. John Oldfield, an
adamant Puritan, lived there from
1650 to 1662, when he was ejected
from the living for refusing to sign
the Act of Uniformity. From 1919,
Edward 'Teddy' Webster ran it as a
post office, but it closed in the
1970s.

A buffet supper was held at Hopton Hall in May 1971, to celebrate the twenty-fifth anniversary of the WI who, in those days, held their meetings at the hall. In the back row, from left to right: Mrs D. Webster, Mrs B. Arnold, Mrs B. Corbett, Mrs A. Lawley, and Mrs K. Marriott. In the middle row: Mrs E. Robinson, Mrs J. Brown, Mrs C. Matkin, Mrs K. Matkin, Miss N. Dakin, Mrs D. Bacon, Mrs M. Repton, Mrs A. Stevenson, and Mrs A. Gell. In the front row: Miss E. Ollerenshaw, Mrs M. Monger, Miss G. Chevons, Mrs E. Dakin, Mrs V. Cochrane, Mrs M. Langley, and Mrs G. Fearn.

Hopton Hall grounds around the turn of the century with local people gathering for a special event.

Hopton Hall, looking towards what is now Carsington Reservoir, in the 1950s. The sixteenth-century hall was the home of the Gell family for nearly five centuries. The contents of the house were finally sold in 1989.

The WI, celebrating their fortieth birthday at the Waterloo Inn, near Taddington, in 1986. They are, from the left: Mrs E. Senior, Mrs D. Bacon, Mrs M. Repton, Mrs M. Ward, Mrs K. Matkin, Mrs A. Andrews, Mrs A. Stevenson, Mrs K. Marriott, Mrs M. Hutchinson, Mrs E. Horrocks, Mrs M. Monger, Mrs E. Moss, Mrs J. Brown, Mrs M. Oldfield, and Mrs H. Parkin.

Carsington and Hopton primary school, in 1930. In the back row, from left to right: Pat Repton, Eric Ward, John Matkin, Fred Glossop, Don Matkin, Victor Travis, Lionel Matkin, and Miss Maddocks. In the middle row: Gladys Travis, Beatrice Bacon, Mary Taylor, Mabel Maskrey, and Betty Taylor. In the front row: Majorie Travis, Freda Heathfield, Evelyn Smith, Dorothy Wigley and Jean Repton. The school was built in 1726 and has been much restored in the twentieth century. There is a plaque on the west wall inscribed 'This school was built and given by Mr Temperance Gell of Hopton for twenty poor children of Hopton and Carson, to learn to read, write and other proper works. Anno Dom. 1726'.

Looking up the main street in Hognaston in the early part of the century. The man in the picture is standing in front of the Red Lion; next door lived Francis Stafford who carried on a tailoring business in the village until 1963, having established the business in 1827. In 1922, the building shown projecting forward above Mr Stafford's house was demolished and George Bembridge set up a bakery business. At one time the street was on the main route from London to Manchester and is the only road marked on the map of Derbyshire compiled by John Ogilby in 1675.

A well dressing outside Rose Cottage, Hognaston, early in the 1900s. Before mains water was piped to the village in the 1930s, the school caretaker used to fetch a bucket of water from the well every day so that the children could wash their hands. The village wells were called into use again during the drought of 1976.

The front yard of Knowl House, Hognaston, with Margaret Steeples standing in front of the pump, c. 1934. The pump still remains today, in a modified form, but the cobblestones have gone.

Hognaston Church of England school was built in memory of Mrs Bunting's husband, at a cost of £400, in 1871. This picture is from around 1912. On the front row, from left to right: Florence Redfern, Evelyn Redfern, Doris Webster, Walter Redfern, and Charles Allsopp. In the second row: James Steeples, Jack Redfern, Percy Webster, Fanny Webster, Louie Bembridge, Robert Allsopp, Clifford Smith, and Polly Frost. On the third row: George Bown, Alex Webster, Edwin Webster, Philip Webster, Sam Redfern, Sidney Renshaw, Dan Allsopp, Richard Hayes, and Phoebe Cooper. On the fourth row: Miss Calladine (infant teacher), Mabel Webster, Alice Litchfield, Nellie Cooper, Ethel Redfern, Ethel Radford, Alice Webster, Hilda Jeffrey, and Miss Slater (headmistress). On the back row: Connie Radford, Elsie Renshaw, Evelyn Webster, Nellie Bown, Mabel Jeffery and Nellie Redfern.

An anniversary weekday service and tea party outside the Methodist church, Hognaston, in 1912. The well is behind the ice-cream stall.

112

The new Congregational chapel, Hognaston, before the extension was built to house the Sunday school, in 1930. The chapel itself was built in 1882.

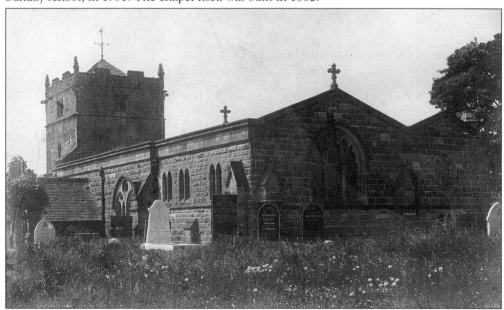

Parts of St Bartholomew's church at Hognaston date back to the twelfth century, although it was largely rebuilt in 1879 by R.F. Robinson of Derby. The vicar at the time was Thomas O'Grady. The clock and three bells were presented by the famous Derby firm of clockmakers, John Smith and Sons, and installed in 1911 as a memorial to John Smith who was born in the village.

Pupils of Hognaston Church of England school, in 1931. In the front row, from left to right: Graham Russell, Roy Watson, Kenneth Hardy, Bill Frost, Horace Dykes, and Ron Russell. In the second row: Esther Bown, Mary Stafford, Nancy Stafford, Joan Dykes, Gordon Bown, Dorothy Bembridge, Audrey Steeples, Dorothy Riley, and May Heathcote. On the third row: Amy Watson, Vera Riley, Phylis Watson, May Ollerenshaw, Maud Frost, Edna Bembridge, Florrie Frost, Mary Dykes, Dorothy Frost, and Bill Riley. In the back row: Miss Knowles, Cyril Bembridge, Frank Frost, John Heathcote, Eddie Frost, Clem Bembridge, Tom Bown, Arthur Bembridge, Alan Russell, and Miss Hall (later Mrs Watson). The school closed in 1981, with only seven children on the roll.

John and Helen Bembridge outside Knowl House, which was built in 1694. They established a bakery business from the house at the turn of the century. There were three bakeries in Hognaston at one time, to meet the needs of the local communities. Note the yoke on the wall.

Haymaking in Holy Trinity churchyard, Kirk Ireton, in 1969. Ralph Kelsey is on the left and Luke Wood on the right. Apart from his duties keeping the churchyard tidy, Mr Wood was also a gravedigger and farmer. In his spare time he acted as village barber, using his farm buildings for the purpose. The church, which was built in the twelfth century, was re-roofed in 1973. It has a low Norman tower and is reached through an interesting pair of early eighteenth-century gateposts which are believed to have come from the old manor house.

The Barley Mow, Kirk Ireton, c. 1918, a lofty, gabled, Jacobean building erected in 1683. It is one of the very few remaining old English pubs to have retained the traditional image of what a public house used to look like in times past. Tradition at the Barley Mow was so strong that when decimal coinage was introduced in 1971, the owner, Mrs Ford refused to accept the new currency. Customers had to pay in 'old money' up to the time of her death in 1977.

Kirk Ireton Wakes, with Neville Dean leading the procession past Northfield Farm on the way around the village, in the 1930s. Of the many events that took place at the Wakes, one of the most popular was bowling for the pig. The lucky winner took home a real live pig for company!

Kirk Ireton Mothers' Union pictured on a visit to Josiah Wedgewood and Sons Ltd, Barlaston factory in the 1950s. In the front row, from left to right: Mrs L. Ford, Miss Matkin, Mrs M. Dean, Mrs E. Hallows, Mrs Ward, and Mrs Hadfield. The ladies appear to have been accompanied by one rather camera-shy youngster on the back row.

A mock wedding being performed, as part of the village wakes activities, by Kirk Ireton children, in the 1930s. The bride and groom appear to be taking the event very seriously. In the back row, from left to right: John Allsop, George Ward, Raymond Smedley, and Laurie Ford. In the front row: Elsie Ward, Dorothy Ward, Ron Mould, Lucy Bates, Agnes Dean, and Elsie Kinder. At the rear is Bernard Linthwaite, and Sarah Sherwin (in the doorway).

The Old School House on Well Bank, Kirk Ireton, in the 1950s, with Mrs Whittaker, who lived there, looking over the wall. At the beginning of the century, villagers used to collect water from the two wells on Well Bank. However, in about 1905, water began to be pumped from a reservoir on Blackwall Lane making Kirk Ireton the first village in the Ashbourne Rural District Council area to have its own piped water supply.

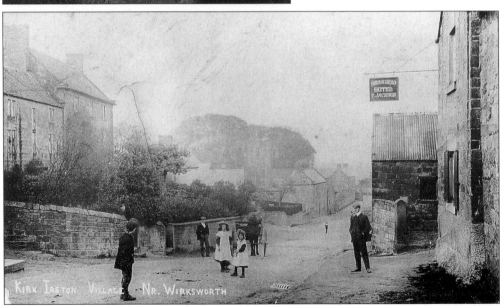

Looking down Main Street, Kirk Ireton in the early 1900s. The Bull's Head, on the right, is now closed. The village rises to about 850 feet above sea-level, with the upper end being known as The Windmill. This is because of the existence, at one time, of a post mill, traces of which were found in recent times. Most of the houses were built of sandstone quarried locally, near to Callow.

Rock Cottage, Kirk Ireton c. 1943. Pictured, from left to right, are: Agnes Dean, Lance Dean (baby in arms), Elizabeth Millington, Marion Dean. At the front is John Millington. Rock Cottage was situated on Coffin Lane, which was, reputedly, the route that coffins took into the village on their way to the church.

The Women's Institute, probably celebrating an anniversary at the Church Institute, Kirk Ireton. Cutting the cake is Mrs Blackwall the president, the wife of Major Blackwall.

Eleven
Middleton

The Basin on The Green, before 1906. Water was a very scarce commodity and had to be severely rationed in times of drought. When Joe Harrison was a water bailiff and drought conditions existed, families were allowed only two buckets of water per day for drinking, cooking and washing. Apart from his job as water bailiff, Mr Harrison also dug graves – a remarkable fact since he was a cripple and used a crutch to support himself. On the extreme right of the picture is the old Primitive Methodist chapel, and next to that the slaughterhouse – both have been demolished. Mount Zion Primitive Methodist chapel was built on the site of the thatched cottage, c. 1906.

An early motor car on the streets of Middleton, outside Harry Flint's shop, formerly Walter Gregson's. In the 1920s, there was a petrol pump available outside The Nelson public house, higher up the street, although there were few customers for it at the time.

The Basin, showing Water Lane to the left, in the early 1900s. It was built for use as a horse trough and was placed there in about 1768, where it remained until it became the victim of a council road widening scheme.

Main Street, Middleton, with Walter Gregson's grocery shop on the left, next to the post office, in the early 1900s. The man in the centre is standing at a popular meeting point for the men folk of the village at the time, to exchange tales. The road in those days was rather rough and winding, but now, following the demolition of some of the buildings, most of the bends have been removed.

A happy group of people on The Green, Middleton, proudly displaying their patriotism on the occasion of King George V's visit to the village on his way to Chatsworth House, c. 1934.

A party of mothers, fathers and other relations assembled to have their photographs taken with their children at a village event.

Irene Brooks, Middleton's Carnival Queen, c. 1930. Irene, was a local girl who lived in Main Street, and her parents were Adam and Maria Brooks who kept a little shop opposite the school, which sold tobacco and sweets to the quarrymen. She later became a nurse.

Middleton Victoria Silver Prize Band, at Middleton vicarage garden party, in 1934. In those days the band played at all of Derby County's home matches at the Baseball Ground until the police band took over in 1937. The most recent notable achievement for the band, following amalgamation with Wirksworth and Brassington bands, was winning the National Brass Band (Midland Region) Championships in April 1974. In the back row, from left to right: Walter Spencer, Arthur Else, Billy Evans, Jadda Houghton, Bill Statham, Herbert Hallows, and Jack Doxey Jnr. In the second row: Mr Spencer, J.S. Batterley, Mr Cordin, Sam Pearson, John Doxey, Mr Killer, W. Evans, and Albert Slack. In the front row: W. Else, J. Doxey Snr, Alec Spencer, J.S. Spencer, Mr Cottell, Jim Benson, Mr Mather, and W. Jones.

Judging by the numbers, a large percentage of the male population turned up for this meeting, in the mid 1930s. Middleton Church Hall, as it was known then, is at the rear.

Mountain Cottage, looking down on the Via Gellia, where D.H. Lawrence lived with his German born wife Frieda, in 1918. They had been pressured into leaving Cornwall by the local authorities, who thought she had been spying on shipping movements for the enemy.

Middleton school, 1910. Front row, left to right: Frank Tyms, William Tyms, Sidney Flint, Billy Flint, Harry Gregson, William Boden. The list of names for the remaining children is incomplete but we know that the second row includes: Joe Spencer, Annie Walker, Sarah Ann Spencer, Ethel Hallows, Mervyn Killer. The third row includes: Sarah Buckley, Grace Else, Ivy Hallows, Doris Birley, Violet Fox, Winnie Birley, Billy Slack. The back row includes: Charlie Spencer, Sam Slack, Joe Walker, Harold Slack, Andrew Martin. The teachers are Miss Ann Buckley (left) and Miss Dryborough.

The Happy Wanderers second annual pantomime, in 1973, was *Rumpelstiltskin*, for which the stage was specially extended to allow the cast more room to perform. On the back row, from left to right: Graham Millward (Loony Lennie), Irene Holmes (Prince Hal of Debonnaire), Deric Longden (Balderdash), Trevor Oswald (Bunkum), and Paul Wolfenden (Dame Daffodil). On the front row: Lynne Todd (Hound Oozie), Wendy Hepplewhite (Rumpelstilskin), Pat Doxey (Annette), and Ted Fowke (King Krustaceous of Kornovia). Deric Longden is now a well-known writer and broadcaster.

Middleton Church Hall was built *c.* 1927. In the picture, a party of workers apply some finishing touches, with the Revd Cottle in the foreground. Village people of all denominations helped in the building and fund raising for the hall and there was a great deal of controversy when it was called Middleton Church Hall. This has been laid to rest in recent years since, following modernisation, it is now called Middleton Village Hall.

The cast of *Jack and the Beanstalk*, in 1972. This was the first pantomime to be put on by the Happy Wanderers. Despite the threatened power cuts, the philosophy that the show must go on was adopted and emergency lighting was provided for back up purposes. The producer was Roger Southam, who also took the part of the widow. Graham Millward was Daffy Doddle, Jack was played by Irene Holmes and his girl friend by Pat Doxey. Cyril Moore was the giant, Ted Fowke the bailiff, and Ann Holmes and Carol Hopkins played the demon and the fairy.

Middleton football club, pictured after winning the Alfreton and District Football League, c. 1982. On the back row, from left to right: John Doxey (committee man), Barrie Price (chairman), Mark Holloway, David Pearson, Chris Beckett, Trevor Wright, Alan Pearson, Chris Baker, Keith Campion, Cedric Pearson (secretary), and Joe Maskery (manager). On the front row: Rob Inglis, Kevin Wagstaff, Tony Holloway, Colin Julian, and Michael Doxey. Further honours came the club's way in 1991, when they were champions of the Derby City League and also won the League Cup.

The Happy Wanderers float depicting pantomime characters, which won first prize in the fancy dress tableaux at Wirksworth Carnival in 1972. In the back row, from left to right: Linda Dickinson, Peter Wilkinson, Irene Holmes, and Ted Fowke. In the front row: Kath Alesbrook, Pat Allsop, Karin Steube and Gillian Prince.